Car~~~~ ~~~~~~~~

What They Do, How to Become One, and

What the Future Holds!

Brian Rogers

KidLit-O Books

www.kidlito.com

© 2013. All Rights Reserved.

Cover lamge © Sven Vietense - Fotolia.com

Table of Contents

About KidCaps

KidLit-O is an imprint of BookCaps™ that is just for kids! Each month BookCaps will be releasing several books in this exciting imprint. Visit are website or like us on Facebook to see more!

A lawyer presenting evidence to a jury[1]

[1]   Image   source: http://www.howmuchcost.org/wp-content/uploads/2013/01/How-Much-Does-a-Lawyer-Cost.jpg

Introduction

The Chief Counsel for the NAACP, attorney
Thurgood Marshall, stood nervously on May 17,
1954. He had finished his arguments in the case
of *Brown vs. Board of Education* and now he
was about to find out whether or not all of his
hard work had been for nothing. He watched
silently as the nine judges of the United States
Supreme Court came walking into the courtroom
and as they sat down at their seats. The judges,
dressed in long black gowns, looked terribly
serious and avoided eye contact with anyone
standing in front of them in the large courtroom.

These Supreme Court Justices listened to Thurgood Marshall argue the *Brown vs. Board of Education* case in 1954[2]

Chief Justice Earl Warren cleared his throat before he began to speak. The moment had come for the nine justices (as judges on the Supreme Court are called) to announce their decision. For a moment, it seemed to Thurgood Marshall that time itself stood still. His mind started to flash back to the events that had led to this moment.

He could remember the first time that he argued a case before the Supreme Court, way back in 1940. The NAACP (National Association for the Advancement of Colored People) had been hugely impressed with his performance and had made him their chief counsel, or primary lawyer. As an African-American man himself, Thurgood Marshall was thrilled that he would be able to put his law training and trial experience to use on behalf of the African American community as a whole. Now, fourteen years later, here he was representing a group of African-American parents from Kansas, South Carolina, Virginia, and Delaware who wanted to end the segregation of schools in their state. In other words, these parents wanted their African American children to study together with the local white children and not to be treated differently.

Thurgood Marshall had studied the law and he knew that a previous Supreme Court decision from 1896 (in the case of *Plessy vs. Ferguson*) had made it legal for states to segregate schools, restaurants, buses, and even churches. However, Thurgood Marshall (and many others like him) felt that segregation, even if the facilities were equal, made African Americans feel like they weren't as good as other Americans who had a different skin color. The NAACP also that segregation was wrong and so they took the case all the way to the Supreme Court.

As he stood behind the counsel's table, far away from the people that he represented, Thurgood Marshall tried to look at the judges and to guess what their decision might be. He was surprised to see Justice Robert H. Jackson who had recently suffered a heart attack. The fact that Justice Jackson had made the effort to be present for the reading of the decision could be either a good thing or a bad thing. Some people had said that Justice Jackson supported the practice of segregation and didn't feel that the Supreme Court had the right to change that. But here he was, having come directly from the hospital, which meant that he wanted to be present for this important decision.

To Thurgood Marshall's right, the lawyers for the various states' Boards of Education were probably thinking thoughts remarkably similar to his. Once all nine justices were seated, everyone in the courtroom sat down, and Thurgood Marshall found himself holding his breath as the moment of truth arrived.

Chief Justice Warren began to read the prepared statement that would officially announce the decision of the Supreme Court in this important case. After reviewing the basics of the case and talking about the careful research done by and the heated arguments had by the Justices while trying to come to a decision, Chief Justice Warren finally read out loud the unanimous decision (which meant that all nine justices agreed): "Segregation of white and colored children in public schools has a detrimental (negative) effect upon the colored children."[3]

Thurgood Marshall breathed a sigh of relief. He had done it. Together with his legal team, he had successfully argued the *Brown vs. Board of Education* case and helped to take the first step towards ending segregation in the United States. This small group of lawyers, Marshall, his team, and the nine Supreme Court Justices, had worked together to use the law of the land to improve the lives of millions of African Americans and to make the United States a nation where everyone was truly equal, no matter what the color of their skin was.

Can you imagine how it felt to have been a part of the team that argued *Brown vs. Board of*

[3] Quotation source: http://www.ourdocuments.gov/doc.php?flash=true&doc=87&page=transcript

Education before the Supreme Court? Going to sleep that night, surely all of those people who had been involved felt truly satisfied and happy to have been a part of making history.

Today, lawyers across the country are working hard, just like Thurgood Marshall did, to help their clients understand and take advantage of the law. In some cases, lawyers may even have the privilege to assist politicians create new laws!

Have you ever thought about what it would be like to be a lawyer? Do you think that you have what it takes? Well, you probably have some questions about what being a lawyer is all about. And even though you may have seen movies or television shows that talk about what lawyers do, chances are that there is a lot about being a lawyer that you still don't know. In this handbook, we will look at the career of a lawyer from seven different angles in seven intriguing sections.

Each of these sections will tell us something new about lawyers and will help us to see what their lives are actually like.

The first section will tell us some basic facts about lawyers and what they do. While you may only think of lawyers as people who argue important cases before a judge and jury, in reality there are all types of lawyers and some of them hardly ever set foot in a courtroom! We will find out why lawyers are so crucial in a democratic government, what kind of money they make, and why some people say that they have truly flexible job opportunities.

In the second section, we will have a closer look at the training required to become a lawyer. Do you know how many years a lawyer must go to school for and how many distinct kinds of tests they must take? We will also learn why the first year of law school is the hardest for many students.

The third section of this handbook will answer the question: "Is being a lawyer an easy job?" You can probably guess that the answer is no, and you would be right. We will look at three unique conditions that lawyers must deal with almost every day and why those three conditions can make their job quite challenging at times.

Then we will have a look at an average day in the life of a lawyer. Although there are lots of different kinds of lawyers, all of them follow a similar routine each day and must carry out some of the same tasks. While not every moment of a lawyer's life is filled with courtroom drama, what they do is still hugely important for the people that they work with.

The fifth section will show us why being a lawyer is not for everyone. All lawyers must deal with three very difficult realities. Do you think that you will be able to overcome these difficult circumstances and go on to be a successful lawyer anyway? You will be able to decide for yourself after reading this section.

The sixth section will show us what the future holds for the career of a lawyer. Will there be lots of job opportunities for lawyers in the future and will there be any new technology to help them be even more effective at their jobs? We will find out.

Finally, the seventh section will tell you what you can do now to prepare yourself for a career as a lawyer. Although you must graduate high school before beginning your education to be a lawyer, there are lots of things that you can do in the meantime. We will examine the skills, qualities, and activities that you should focus on to help guarantee your success in this exciting career.

Lawyers are known the world over for dressing well, for speaking clearly, and for being the type of people who truly make a difference. Although not everybody thinks that lawyers are essential to society, in reality law professionals play a tremendously important role in each community that they work in. Without them, the world would be a truly different (and more dangerous) place.

Let's learn more about this exciting career!

Chapter 1: What Does a Lawyer Do?

Lawyers must read lots and lots of books about court cases and laws in order to help their clients[4]

---

[4] Image source: http://lawyerlondonontario.com/

When most people think of lawyers, they imagine a person banging their fists down on a table as they try to convince a jury or a judge that their client is innocent or that a certain defendant is guilty. People might imagine the lawyer introducing pieces of evidence and using persuasive arguments to get everyone in the courtroom to agree with their point of view. But in reality, lawyers do much more than just argue in courtrooms. What exactly does a lawyer focus on?

Simply put, lawyers work hard to help people to understand and obey the law. The laws written by local and federal governments can be pretty complicated and hard to understand sometimes. Worse yet, unless a person has read every single part of the law, they can make serious mistakes that may cost them lots of money or even send them to jail! Lawyers help people to understand the parts of the law that have to do with their particular situation and to make sure that others don't take advantage of innocent folks.

In every democratic government (a government where the citizens get to create the laws), lawyers help to protect the citizens both from the government and from each other. They help citizens to have a real influence on how things are done in their country. For example, think about how different things in the United States would be today if Thurgood Marshall wouldn't have been allowed to argue the *Brown vs. Board of Education* case.

But not all lawyers spend their days in courtrooms arguing before juries and judges. In fact, most lawyers hardly ever even see the inside of a courtroom during an average day at work. So what do most lawyers do all day?

There are many different types of lawyers, and each of them plays an important role in their community. Some are **trial lawyers** (like Thurgood Marshall), who focus on representing clients in court cases. They may be **District Attorneys** who work for the government and try to put guilty people in jail, or they may be **defense attorneys** who make sure that the accused person gets a fair trial.

Other lawyers are **corporate attorneys** who work for large companies in tall buildings and help the companies to understand and obey the law. Some of these attorneys eventually practice **international law**, which focuses on helping companies and individuals from different countries to settle their differences and to carry on business.

Some lawyers focus on **real estate**, which has to do with buying and selling properties. They make sure that both the buyers and the sellers use the correct paperwork, handle money properly, and obey the laws of the local government so that there are no problems with the deal. A real estate lawyer is especially valuable when the property being transferred is worth millions of dollars.

Some lawyers work on protecting the **environment**, and their jobs might involve investigating companies that pollute, suing the companies that break pollution laws, and trying to get new laws passed that better protect nature. Other lawyers help clients with personal matters, like **divorces**, **child custody decisions**, **making a will**, **adoptions**, **paying taxes**, **solving problems with a landlord**, and so on.

In every case, lawyers work exceptionally hard to give their clients good advice so that these can make the right decision. Really, that is the main job of a lawyer: to give people good advice. In many cases, lawyers are called "counselors" because they give "counsel" to the people that they are working with. Lawyers who are darned good at their jobs might choose to eventually become **law professors** and **judges**.

What kind of money do lawyers make as they help their clients? While it depends of the specific type of lawyer, in the United States the average lawyer makes about $130,000 per year. However, if they work at a private practice suing large companies, they may be allowed to keep a percentage of each settlement (the money the client gets from the company) which, in some situations, may mean millions of dollars per case. Lawyers who open up big law firms often make hundreds of thousands of dollars per year. But, like most jobs, the enormous salaries don't come right away- they must be earned over time and after lots of hard work.

Lawyers have ultra flexible job opportunities in the sense that they can choose whether to work for a large company or in a small office. They can represent a multi-national corporation and travel the world or can focus on solving the problems of just one person. They can fight to save the earth or even to protect the democratic way of life. There are so many ways to be a lawyer that it seems that there is something for practically everyone.

Lawyers are acutely hardworking people who fight hard to make sure that everyone around them gets an equal chance to make their voice heard.

Chapter 2: What Is the Training Like to Become a Lawyer?

Law students must study lots of different subjects during law school[5]

---

[5] Image source: http://people.howstuffworks.com/becoming-a-lawyer5.htm

The training to become a lawyer can last for up to seven (or sometimes eight) years. During that time, students must study hard and learn to take in lots and lots of information in a short amount of time. So what is the training process like to become a lawyer?

1) Graduate from high school with a high GPA and SAT score

2) Graduate from a four year college with a high GPA

3) Get a good score on the LSAT

4) Choose a specialty and graduate from law school

5) Pass the state bar exam

6) Find a job

Let's have a closer look at each of these steps.

1) Graduate from high school with a high GPA and SAT score. All those who want to go to a four year college need to have graduated from high school. But does that mean that lawyers can take it easy during high school and just try to get passing grades? Not at all. In high school, a student's grades will be added up and then a special number (called a GPA or Grade Point Average) will be calculated. Most colleges require a minimum GPA (normally a 3.0 or higher) which means that future lawyers must have pretty decent grades even in high school in order to get into a good college. Colleges are also interested in the student's score on the SAT (Scholastic Assessment Test) that students take during their final year of high school. A SAT score of at least 1200 (out of 1600) is considered competitive.

2) Graduate from a four year college with a high GPA. After the student has been accepted into a four year college, they must work tremendously hard to get a Bachelor's degree. And as was the case with high school, students must maintain a high GPA in order to be accepted into law school later on. For most law specialties, it doesn't matter too much what subject the student studies during college. The most important thing is that the student gets good grades. For that reason, some experts recommend choosing a subject that you are interested in so that you will be motivated to study hard. Choosing a difficult subject just because it looks good on paper might mean a lower GPA and trouble getting into law school later on.

3) Get a good score on the LSAT. As they get close to finishing their four years in college, the student must pass a special exam called the LSAT (Law School Admission Test). The purpose of the LSAT is to make sure that the student has good reading, writing, and analytical abilities. A score of at least 150 (out of 180) is considered competitive. Law schools pay a lot of attention to a student's GPA during college and to their score on the LSAT.

4) Choose a specialty and graduate from law school. Did you see the list of subjects at the beginning of this section? During their first year, law students must study a lot of information. In fact, most laws schools (which last from three to four years) require that students study the same basic information, although it may or may not have anything to do with the specialty that the students will eventually want to practice. The idea is that the information studied during the first year will serve as a foundation for the student's further studies. Like a tall building that must be built on solid ground, good lawyers must understand the basics of the law before they can focus on anything more specific. During their second and third years, a student can choose which courses they want to take and start to focus on one specific area of law practice.

5) Pass the state bar exam. Once they have graduated from law school with a J.D. degree

("Juris Doctor" or "Doctor of Law") a lawyer must prove that they have enough knowledge of laws and legal procedures to start practicing what they have learned. Most states have a special group of lawyers who prepare a test that each new lawyer must pass. Called a "state bar exam", these tests are usually made up of essay questions where a new lawyer must describe how he or she would handle a certain legal situation and why they would choose certain methods or tactics. The state wants to see that new lawyers know how to reason on a case, how to pay attention to all the facts, and how to use the laws properly to work out solutions to complicated problems. After a lawyer has passed the state bar exam, they are officially allowed to practice law in that state.

6) Find a job. Once lawyers are certified to practice law in their state, they must go out and try to find a job. They might use special connections to get a job where they already know someone or they might send out their résumé (a description of their education and abilities) to different companies in the area who are looking for a lawyer. Sometimes there are more lawyers than jobs available, which means that the competition for those jobs can be pretty tough. But by talking to as many people possible and trying their best to help new employers see how good of a lawyer they are, many law school graduates can find a job soon after passing the state bar exam.

Chapter 3: Is Being a Lawyer An Easy Job?

Sometimes, lawyers feel like they are being buried alive by papers[6]

Lawyers have to study extremely hard in order to graduate from high school, college, and law school. They must also pass a series of important tests (the SAT, LSAT, and State Bar Exam) on the road to becoming a lawyer. But once they have passed all these important tests and have been certified to practice law in their state, does that mean that lawyers can take it easy and just sit back and make lots of money for doing nothing? Not at all. Being a lawyer has some truly unique challenges that can make it a pretty difficult job at times. Let's look at three of these challenges: the long hours, the reading and the research, and the difficult clients.

The long hours. Most lawyers do not work a typical 9-5 schedule. In fact, the amount of work that lawyers have to do simply cannot fit into a normal 40 hour work week. As a result, most lawyers end up working anywhere from 50 to 70

[6] Image source: http://tinyurl.com/ls6m7yr

hours each week, or an average of 10-12 hours per day, often including weekends. Can you imagine spending so much time working?

Lawyers, as part of their job, sometimes have to interview different people to learn information about a certain case. While some interviews can be conducted over the phone, there are occasions when certain information can only be obtained by physically going to meet with the person and speaking with them face to face. Can you imagine spending long days travelling to small towns all across the state (or even country) in order to get the truth about what happened during a certain event?

Successful lawyers love their jobs and have accepted that being a lawyer means working long hours. But others who start this career thinking only about making lots of money soon end up getting tired, angry, and starting to resent their career as a lawyer. The long hours can be terribly difficult for some people to deal with.

<u>The reading and the research.</u> Whenever a lawyer receives a specific task, whether it is to prove the guilt of a suspect, to defend a client, to prepare documents for a business transaction, or something else, they must generally read lots of information and do lots of research. In some cases, they must read hundreds of pages to learn about past cases, looking for details about a previous judge's decision that may help them to complete their current task. Lawyers must research the laws of the area where they are working to make sure that their client doesn't do anything illegal or unethical. Often, much of a lawyer's time is spent sitting at their desk with a big pile of books, looking for one or two little sentences that might help them.

Can you imagine having to read so much information in such a short time, remembering everything that you read and being able to know which information is the most important for each case? Lawyers must learn to sort out information after reading it only once and to remember where to find the answers to their questions. Not everyone has the mental energy or desire to work so hard.

The difficult clients. Lawyers are available to help clients who want to understand the law better or who need help resolving a legal problem with another person or group of people. In many cases, people go to visit a lawyer when they are extremely desperate, scared, or worried. By the time that they finally sit down and speak with a lawyer, the client may be so emotionally worked up that they lose their temper easily, can't express themselves well, or even start blaming the lawyer for their problems. Can you imagine working with people like that?

Lawyers have a lot of pressure put on them to do exactly what the client wants. Unfortunately, it's not always possible to keep the client happy. Sometimes, the lawyer needs several days, weeks, or even months to research and prepare the case, to file documents, or to speak with the necessary witnesses. Clients can easily get impatient and begin to demand results, which can put even more pressure on the lawyer who is already working around the clock to get the job done. As a result of all the stress, some lawyers start to suffer from depression, from heart problems, and some even have trouble sleeping at night. Experienced lawyers have learned to deal with all this stress by exercising, by talking with a trusted friend about their problems, and by managing how much work they allow themselves to take on.

Being a lawyer is by no means an easy job. They must work exceptionally long hours, do a lot of reading and research, and deal from time to time with unreasonable clients. However, for those who learn to cope with these difficulties, a life of rewarding service (and high salaries) awaits them!

Chapter 4: What Is An Average Day Like For a Lawyer?

A lawyer hard at work on an average day[7]

---

[7] Image source: http://findinganattorney.wordpress.com/

There are many different types of lawyers, and some spend of them their time arguing cases in front of juries and judges while others focus on meeting with couples in the middle of a divorce. No matter what their specialty is, though, all lawyers have to carry out the same basic routine each day. Let's look at a few of the most salient parts of an average day at work for a lawyer.

All lawyers must spend most of their time gathering and organizing information. That means conducting interviews (in person or over the telephone), reading case files, and investigating laws and related court decisions. Most law offices have large collections of legal books that cost thousands of dollars. But those collections of books do not simply sit on the shelves gathering dust- they get used very frequently by both lawyers and by their assistants (called "paralegals").

Lawyers also make appointments to have face to face meetings and telephone conferences. Who do they invite to these meetings? Lawyers spend must meet with experts who can give them information about a case and with witnesses who will offer testimony about something that they saw, heard, or know. They must also have regular meetings with their clients to give them updates on the project, to get additional information from them, and to prepare them for the different phases of the legal action. Meetings are also held with fellow lawyers to discuss the cases they are working on and what kinds of strategies might help them to do what the clients want. Trial lawyers also spent time negotiating, meeting with judges, and arguing their cases in a courtroom.

Lawyers also spend lots of time writing. They must prepare documents that meet the legal standards for the area that they are working in, including deeds, wills, adoption papers, settlements, and purchase agreements. Special motions (requests) must be filed during some court cases as well as warrants and witness requests (called "summons"). Reports of each case and special notes must also be gathered, put into a file, and stored in a place where they will be easy to find again. Lawyers also spend time organizing these completed case files so that they can easily locate information about past cases or clients whenever they need it.

While the average lawyer may start work at the same time as most everyone else, around eight o'clock in the morning, they usually stay at their offices long after the rest of the world has gone home. They read, file, write, make phone calls, visit witnesses, meet with clients, and have telephone conferences while the rest of the world is at home watching TV or relaxing with their friends and family. When they finally get to bed, lawyers sometimes find that their heads are so full of facts and figures that it takes them a while to fall asleep.

Chapter 5: What Is the Hardest Part of Being a Lawyer?

Sometimes, a lawyer may feel like a professional juggler with too many balls in the air[8]

As we have seen, lawyers are very important people. They make sure that even the little guy's voice is heard. A lot of people are impressed when they meet a lawyer because these law

---

[8] Image source: http://careerdirectionsllc.com/secrets-to-juggling-job-offers/

professionals are smart, dress well, and make lots of money. But, if being a lawyer is so great and they are so well-respected and well-paid, why aren't more people working as lawyers? Well, the truth is that there are some particularly difficult aspects of a career as a lawyer. Let's look at three working conditions that are so tough that some people have decided that they could never deal with them and that being a lawyer just isn't their cup of tea.

First, lawyers must try to <u>balance their work with the rest of their life</u>. Why can it be so hard to balance the different parts of their life? Let's make a comparison. Have you ever tried juggling balls? A lot of kids like to grab three balls and try to keep all three in the air at the same time. In order to juggle well, you have to have a good eye and quick reflexes. But have you ever seen a professional juggler who can juggle four, five, six, or even more balls at the same time? In a way, lawyers often feel like jugglers. How so?

Lawyers have a lot of responsibilities at their jobs. They must work long hours to give the best advice and service to their clients. As we saw earlier, many law firms expect their lawyers to work anywhere from 50 to 70 hours per week in order to keep both the firm and the clients happy. However, when can that kind of a schedule become a problem?

Think about the effect that a lawyer's job has on their families and friends. How do you think that they feel about the lawyer spending so much time at the office? Do you think that the lawyer's husband or wife misses being with them sometimes? Of course! And how does the situation change when the lawyer has children or wants to be active in a club, in sports, or in their religion? How will they ever find time for it all? When will they have time to fix things around the house, to take the car to the mechanic, to go shopping, and to spend time with their extended family? Really, each person on earth only has 24 hours a day to spend doing the things that they have to do. Lawyers have chosen to spend most of those 24 hours per day working at their jobs. But while their jobs are hugely important, they know that other things and people in their lives are also extremely beneficial. Not everyone is good at learning how to balance the responsibilities of a job with the responsibilities of an adult life. This constant juggling act has been enough to make some people say "no" to a career as a lawyer.

Second, the work of most lawyers has a big impact on the lives of others. Trial lawyers determine whether or not a person ends up in jail; divorce lawyers determine how much money each side will be left with, and corporate lawyers might make a small mistake that leads to the shutdown of a large company and the loss of thousands of jobs. Not every person can deal with the often extreme stress of knowing that so many lives are affected by the way that they work. In some cases, lawyers may even be attacked by the people who lost something because of them. So how do successful lawyers keep focused and productive despite these often difficult working conditions?

A big help for lawyers is to try and remember that, while they may have a negative impact on the lives of some people, they can also have a tremendously positive impact on the lives of many others. For example, think again of Thurgood Marshall, the attorney who argued the *Brown vs. Board of Education* case before the United States Supreme Court. While Thurgood Marshall didn't want to lose the case and disappoint everyone he was representing, he didn't let his fears keep him from stepping into that courtroom and arguing his case. What motivated him? He surely thought about all of the people that his hard work would help if he was successful.

Third, lawyers must live with <u>a lot of debt</u> after finishing their studies. All during college and law school, most lawyers are so focused on their education that they aren't able to earn any money working at a part time job. They may have some savings or financial help that lets them pay for a place to live, for something to eat, and to take care of transportation costs. But after spending seven years or more buying books and paying high tuitions, many lawyers graduate with anywhere from $72,000 to $100,000 worth of debt that needs to be paid off after they graduate. Can you imagine owing anyone so much money? Do you think that it would stress you out if you couldn't find a job right away?

While being a lawyer is an important and respectable job, these three difficult working conditions have made some people decide that the career of a lawyer is not their cup of tea. However, if, after looking at the nature of the job realistically, you think that you can still be a lawyer, then don't let any fears or negative thoughts hold you back!

Chapter 6: What Does the Future Hold for Lawyers?

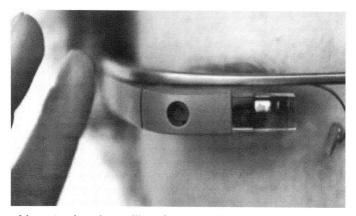

New technology like Google Glass has created new problems that future lawyers will need to solve[9]

---

[9] Image source: http://www.futurelawyer.com/

Lawyers have been around for hundreds of years and have always tried their best to help people understand the law and to solve disputes between citizens. New technologies have helped lawyers to save time and to be more efficient than ever. For example, many case files and law books are now available online and in different computer programs. Instead of having long bookshelves full of heavy books, many modern law offices have a just few computers and an internet connection.

But you may be wondering what the future holds for lawyers? In ten years or so, around the time that you may start down the road towards choosing a career, will the world still need lawyers? What kinds of new technologies and developments may make lawyers even more effective at their jobs? Let's learn the answers to these questions.

Right now, there are thousands lawyers working in cities across the country, and in the future things aren't likely to change. In fact, it has been predicted that, by the year 2020, there will be about 10 percent more opportunities for lawyers than there are today. So while competition will still be pretty tough to get a job as a lawyer, you can be sure that the world will absolutely still need them. In fact, something exciting about practicing law is that there are always new jobs opening up. How so?

Well, as the world changes and new ideas are developed, someone needs to represent those new ideas and to make sure that they are protected. For example, back in the year 1900, remarkably few people were worried about equal rights for white Americans and African Americans. But soon new ideas about equality started to get popular, and lawyers like Thurgood Marshall quickly found work protecting those new ideas. Another example was in the 1990s when news stations across the country began to closely follow famous court cases and began to hire lawyers as "legal experts" to explain what was happening in those court cases. Yet another example was seen when musicians like Metallica and Dr. Dre began to hire lawyers in the early 2000s to protect their music from being illegally downloaded on the internet.

The point is that as new ideas appear lawyers are quick to offer their services. One hundred years ago, there were no jobs for civil rights lawyers, cable news legal experts, or for lawyers fighting digital music piracy. Today, those jobs exist and keep many lawyers busy all day long. In the future, even more new ideas will be developed and will need to be protected by lawyers. New technology will give lawyers plenty to do and will even change the way that they work.

For example, look at the picture at the beginning of this section. Can you recognize that new invention? It is a miniature camera that can be worn like glasses on a person's head and can be connected to the internet. The device allows the person wearing it to make phone calls, surf the internet, record video with sound, and to take pictures by just speaking the right command. This new device, called Google Glass, sounds pretty groovy, but it has a lot of people worried about privacy. After all, a person using this device could record anyone without their knowledge and could post videos or photos on the internet without anyone's permission. In the future, lawyers will have to work hard to control how this new technology is used and how the freedom of the user can be balanced with the right to privacy of the people around that user.

Some experts also think that computers and the internet will change the way that court cases are conducted. Right now, everyone has to get dressed up and must personally appear before a judge and/or jury during their trial. In some areas, though, judges are beginning to sentence certain criminals without ever actually meeting them in person. How do they do it? They use an internet connection and a video conferencing system to speak with the convicted criminals. But in the future, this technology may be used even more. In his book *Tomorrow's Lawyers: An Introduction to Your Future*, author Richard Susskind writes about a future where entire trials will be held online and where the judge, lawyers, defendants, and juries may all be in separate buildings or even in different towns![10] Can you imagine speaking to a judge or jury without ever leaving your house?

Technology has already helped lawyers to find valuable information more quickly and to stay in contact with clients even when travelling or

---

[10] Information source: http://www.amazon.com/Tomorrows-Lawyers-Introduction-Your-Future/dp/019966806X

working from home. However, in the future, technology will create new problems that will need new solutions. We can be sure that lawyers will be there to help us survive the growing pains.

Chapter 7: How Can You Get Ready Now To Be a Lawyer?

While kids can't be lawyers, there are a lot of things that they can do to prepare themselves[11]

---

[11] Image source: http://www.ehow.com/how_2272813_obtain-minor-emancipation-lawyer.html

As we saw earlier, to start on the path that leads to becoming a lawyer you must have already graduated from high school. For most people, that happens when they are around 18 years old. In the meantime, that is, until you turn 18 and graduate from high school, what can you do to get ready for a life as a lawyer? Let's look at a few practical suggestions.

Lawyers need to have certain skills in order to be successful. We saw how important the skills of reading, writing, and analyzing information are during school and even after graduation. So start now learning how to read lots of information, separating what you learn into sections and deciding which points are the most important ones. Practice your writing skills too, perhaps in a journal, for the school newspaper, or on an online blog.

Aside from book work, lawyers also need to develop other important skills like communicating clearly, controlling their temper when in stressful situations, and speaking in public. How can you develop these skills now? Ask your parents or another trusted adult what tips they can give you about communicating clearly. They may suggest thinking carefully before you speak, organizing your thoughts well, and taking into consideration who your audience is and what they may or may not already know about the subject that you are discussing.

You show that you have control over your temper every time that you refuse to use hurtful words or actions even if another person is saying mean things about you. If you get a part-time job, play organized sports, or spend a lot of time with friends, you will most likely be exposed to different types of personalities and opinions. From time to time, you will probably find that you don't always agree with everything that others say or do. When that happens, learn to control your words and to stay calm. The ability to keep your cool even when under pressure will help you to deal with emotional clients and stressful cases when you start working as a lawyer later on.

But how can you learn to speak in public? Even while you are in school there will most likely be several opportunities for you to practice this skill. Can you run for office, maybe becoming president of your class or school? Can you join the debate team and learn to argue your opinion in front of an audience? Can you be an announcer for sports programs or pep rallies? All of these activities can help you to feel more comfortable speaking in front of large audiences.

You can also try to develop the personality of a lawyer. To be willing to spend long hours practicing law each week, lawyers have to seriously love their job. They have to believe that what they do is important and that it is not just about the money. Lawyers love getting tough assignments and finding a way to finish them on time. They love analyzing the facts and trying to get to the bottom of it all. Does that describe you? If not, are you willing to change your personality a little?

After all, the way that you view your work can make a big difference whether or not you enjoy doing it. Trying to learn to view research and investigation like a sort of treasure hunt and puzzle all rolled into one has helped many lawyers to work effectively at their jobs for decades.

Once you have worked to develop the skills and personality of a successful lawyer, you should start thinking about what college and law school you want to attend. Most experts recommend making three separate lists when looking at schools: 1) The schools you like most but aren't likely to get accepted to; 2) the schools that are nice and more likely to accept you; 3) the schools that will undoubtedly accept you just in case all the schools on the first two lists don't accept your applications.

How can you decide which schools to apply for? First off, talk to your parents, teachers, and guidance counselors at school. They can give you an idea of which colleges and law schools will help you reach your goals. And a few factors that you will want to take into consideration may include where the school is located, how many applications the school accepts each year, if there are any costs for applying to the school, how much tuition and living expenses will cost, and whether or not the degree that you will earn will be recognized in other states.

Take the time to sit down and crunch some numbers. You will probably see that attending school for seven years to become a lawyer is quite expensive. But if you start saving up and looking for the money early, there are ways that you can avoid the large debt that some lawyers end up with. Your school counselor can let you know about government grants (money given to you by the state and/or federal government to help with college), scholarships (given by organizations and schools for students with good grades and behavior) and student loans (money that you have to pay back later). If you plan it out right, you can reduce the cost of school and still get a quality education.

Finally, start learning as much as you can about the different specialties that lawyers can choose to practice. Do you want to travel and work with people who speak different languages and come from different cultures? Then maybe international law is the best choice for you. Do you want to protect wildlife and the ecosystem from polluters and irresponsible people? Then look into practicing environmental law. Do you want to make sure that reckless doctors, drivers, and CEOs don't mistreat others and get away with it? Then open up a private practice and look into filing lawsuits and making bad people pay their victims lots of money. The more you know about the law and the different specialties practiced by lawyers, the better informed you will be later on when you have to choose your own specialty by selecting special courses during your second and third years of law school.

As you can see, there are a lot of things that you can do right now to prepare yourself for life as a lawyer. Develop your skills and personality, and research schools and ways of paying for them. This will give you a head start as you move into the highly-competitive world of college, law school, and beyond.

Conclusion

The exciting life of a lawyer doesn't really get started until after they graduate from law school[12]

[12] Image source: http://efastfacts.com/blog/online-marketing-strategy-for-a-successful-lawyer.html

Wow! We have learned a lot about the exciting and important career of a lawyer. In these seven sections, what was your favorite part? Was it when we talked about Thurgood Marshall and his famous case in the Supreme Court or when we looked at the long process to becoming a lawyer? Let's review some of the most important things that we learned in this handbook so that you don't forget them.

The first section told us about the career of a lawyer. While many people only think of lawyers as people who argue important cases before a judge, in reality we saw that there are all types of lawyers and that some of them hardly ever even set foot in a courtroom! Did you see why lawyers are so important in any democratic government? It is because they are the ones who make sure that all citizens have a share in making the laws and they help them to understand and be protected by the laws of the land. We also saw that the average lawyer makes around $130,000 per year, although some may make much more.

In the second section, we had a closer look at the training required to become a lawyer. Did you see how many years a lawyer has to go to school for? The average lawyer must go to school for at least seven years after leaving high school. In addition to passing all of the tests in their courses, they must do well on the SAT, the LSAT, and the state bar exam. We also saw how during the first year of law school the students must learn large amounts of information on many different subjects to give them a strong foundation for the special courses that they will take later on.

The third section answered the question: "Is being a lawyer an easy job?" As you saw, the answer is no. We looked at three unique conditions that can make the job of a lawyer quite difficult at times. We saw how working long hours, reading and researching lots of information, and dealing with upset clients all can add a special challenge to the work of a lawyer. However, we also how many experienced lawyers have learned to deal with these conditions by exercising, by getting enough rest, and by managing their time better.

Then, in the fourth section, we had a look at an average day for a lawyer. Although there are lots of different types of lawyers, we saw how all of them follow a similar routine each day and must carry out some of the same tasks. They must read, conduct interviews, have meetings with clients and fellow lawyers, prepare paperwork and reports, and file documents. Some lawyers must also appear in court as part of their job, but this is not the case with all lawyers.

The fifth section showed us why being a lawyer is not for everyone. All lawyers must deal with three very difficult circumstances. We saw how all lawyers must learn how to balance the long hours required by their job with other responsibilities in their life and how they must pay off large amounts of debt. We also learned that lawyers must constantly think about how their actions affect the lives of others, especially those lawyers who work with criminals. Lawyers like that often have to worry about the reactions of the criminals and what they might do if they aren't happy with what the lawyer has done. After looking at the dark side of being a lawyer, do you think that you will be able to overcome those difficult circumstances and be a successful attorney?

The sixth section showed us what the future holds for the career of a lawyer. We saw that the world will still need lawyers in the future. New technology will surely make it easier for lawyers to help their clients, but it may also create new problems that lawyers will need to solve. While virtual courtrooms may save a lot of time and money, new inventions like Google Glass may create conflicts that lawyers will have to sort out.

Finally, the seventh section showed you what you can do now to prepare yourself for a career as a lawyer. Although you must graduate high school before beginning your education to become a lawyer, there are lots of things that you can do in the meantime. We saw how developing good reading, writing, and analytical skills can help you to do better in school now and later on as a lawyer. Having the right personality (loving hard work, learning, and investigating) will help to keep you motivated and happy during each and every long work week of a lawyer. And investigating which schools you might apply for in the future can help you to be more certain of reaching your goals and may help you to avoid the large debt that many new lawyers have to deal with.

Ever since governments started to write down their laws, their citizens have needed someone to help them to understand the laws of the land and to make sure that they were protected by them. Today, lawyers continue to have the important job of making sure that the law works for and protects the citizens. It's true that most lawyers charge a lot of money for their services, but that's because they provide advice and experience that would be impossible to get anywhere else.

If you think that you have what it take to become a lawyer, then don't hesitate to start getting ready now. The world needs you!

71447770R00041

Made in the USA
Columbia, SC
26 August 2019